Self-Centeredness: The Source of All Grief

by Andrew Wommack

Self-Centeredness: The Source of All Grief
ISBN ISBN: 978-1-59548-049-1
Copyright © 2012 by Andrew Wommack Ministries, Inc.
850 Elkton Dr.
Colorado Springs, CO 80907

Published by Andrew Wommack Ministries, Inc.

Table of Contents

Jesus or Self?

"Ye have heard how I said unto you, I go away, and come again unto you. If ye loved me, ye would rejoice, because I said, I go unto the Father: for my Father is greater than I" (John 14:28).

The night before His crucifixion, Jesus confronted His disciples saying, "Guys, if you really loved Me, you wouldn't be depressed right now! These feelings have come because you're thinking, *Look what I gave up to be Your disciple—my plans, my hopes, my dreams. Now my fishing business is ruined! What's going to happen to me if You aren't really the Messiah, and if I'm not the foundation of Your Church? Will they crucify me next?* Earlier today you were fighting over which one of you is greatest and worthy of the best seat in the kingdom. Don't be so self-centered! Rejoice that I'm going to My Father!"

Self-centeredness caused their grief. If the disciples had truly loved Jesus more than themselves, they would've rejoiced to hear of Him going to the Father. Instead they mourned over their impending loss, thinking, *The Lord is leaving me. What am I going to do?* The disciples entered into the most challenging time of their lives—Christ's betrayal, arrest, and crucifixion—more concerned about what was happening to them than to Jesus. They were totally consumed with self!

The Lord wants to confront your self-centeredness too! Have you ever consciously dealt with self before? How much of your life is characterized by pride, anger, crisis, and grief? Do you really love the Lord more than you love yourself?

Difficult situations have a way of revealing what's truly in your heart. It doesn't matter if your problem is financial pressure, a relational breakdown, or the death of a loved one; you choose whether it turns into a crisis or not. God's already given you everything you need to overcome in life, but it's up to you to use it!

Will you continue in your selfish life or become a living sacrifice? Jesus or self—the choice is yours!

Chapter One

The Root Issue

Grief is rooted in self-centeredness. When a loved one dies, we tearfully ask ourselves, "How can I go on without them?" Giving in to strong emotions, we focus on the death and loss crying, "I won't ever see them alive on earth again!" We then convince ourselves that our mourning is for the dead, when in reality, it's for ourselves.

If the deceased person you're grieving over was saved and now in heaven, there is much to celebrate. Your loved one now stands in the presence of Jesus receiving their eternal reward! Can you imagine the atmosphere of a believer's funeral if you weren't so self-centered? Instead of crisis, what an exciting time of thanksgiving, praise, and rejoicing it would be!

Truly, your grief comes because of selfishness. Pain and loss seem more real to you than the truth of your loved one's happiness and peace in heaven. Stop and ask yourself, "Why am I really grieving? Is this sorrow for them or for me?" An honest answer will reveal the selfishness in your heart.

Whether you find yourself at a funeral or just in the middle of everyday life, self-centeredness can turn anything into a crisis!

Would You Like to Trade Places?

Have you ever been depressed about your finances? If so, you really have nothing much to grieve about. Most of your crisis situations are only a "crisis" to you. While you gripe about the provision for your "need" not being manifest yet, the people around you wonder, *What's the big deal?* The big deal's just that self-centeredness has magnified your molehill into a mountain. "Both of my televisions are old and beat up—I need a new one!" "I'm disappointed because I can't purchase my new stereo system yet!" "My car is already a year old. It's time to buy another."

Your perspective would change if you reached beyond yourself and your own crisis to help someone else in a more difficult place. Your problems would shrink fast as you pitched in and assisted someone who's been devastated financially, emotionally, spiritually, or physically. All of a sudden, it would dawn on you—*I'm really not as bad off as I thought!*

Kicking the Dead

Self-centered people are easily offended. They find ways to get upset over the simplest and silliest things! Then they proceed down that well traveled path to depression, discouragement, and defeat. Why? They're totally consumed with self!

If you would take a step back and be objective when you start sliding into another crisis, you could save yourself much grief. Ask the hard questions, "Where do I stand in this? Why am I so defeated? Has my self been stepped on?" If you deal with yourself like this when your feathers get ruffled, many of your "crises" would cease to be crises.

Dead people never feel a thing! You can do all kinds of mean things to a corpse without any response. Kick it, spit on it, slap it, do whatever, but it won't retaliate. Why? Because it's dead! According to the Bible, you are supposed to be dead (Rom. 6:8 and 2 Tim. 2:11). Why, then, are you hurt so easily when someone says or does something to you? Why do you have so many problems in your relationships? Plain and simple—pride is still alive!

It's Your Choice

"Only by pride cometh contention" (Prov. 13:10). Are you experiencing bitterness, hurt, or anger? God's Word leaves no room to sidestep your responsibility. You might as well face it sooner rather than later because there's no other reason. You weren't born this way, it's not your personality, and circumstances aren't to blame. Contention came into your life because of pride! Pride is not a leading cause; it's the only cause.

Our prototype, Jesus, lived by faith. He never operated out of pure divinity while here on earth. Christ lived His life before us as a man and by faith in God. While being crucified, He prayed, "Father, forgive them; for they know not what they do" (Luke 23:34). Shortly afterward, Stephen demonstrated man's capacity to do the same. While being stoned to death, he prayed, "Lord, lay not this sin to their charge" (Acts 7:60). Jesus chose to forgive and so must we!

"Be ye kind one to another, tenderhearted, forgiving one another, even as God for Christ's sake hath forgiven you" (Eph. 4:32). The Lord won't command you to do something you can't do. In Him, you have the power to forgive and walk in love toward all people. You've been given the ability—now exercise it by faith!

No-Fault Relationships

Have you ever heard of "no-fault relationships"? Maybe you're more familiar with the term "no-fault car insurance." Loosely, this means no matter who is at fault in a car accident, the insurance company will make sure your medical bills are paid (according to the amount of coverage purchased). Similarly in no-fault relationships you choose to walk in love and forgiveness toward all other people no matter how they treat you. According to Matthew 18:21-22, God's "coverage" is even up to seventy times seven! You can do this because Jesus did, and now He's living His life in and through you!

The world's way is to treat others the way they deserve to be treated. It's familiarly expressed as "Scratch my back and I'll scratch yours!" and "Mess with me and you've got another thing coming!" If we live our lives treating people the way they deserve to be treated, we'll be a mess! Why? People don't deserve to be loved—none of us do! Apart from Jesus, we aren't even worth spitting on! We can compare ourselves to whomever we will, but on our own, we still fall short of the glory of God!

"Andrew, you have traveled all over the world teaching God's Word, healing the sick, and ministering salvation to the lost. You've been filled with the Holy Spirit for decades and have experienced many powerful encounters with God. Surely you have your act together!" I hate to burst your bubble, but I'm as human as you are. Ask my wife—she can tell you! Jamie's seen me at my best, worst, and everything in between. She knows I still have problems!

I don't deserve to be loved! In fact, if my wife gave me what I deserved, she would have divorced me many years ago. Why? I don't take perfect care of her. The Scriptures tell me to love her as Christ loved the church, and I have yet to completely fulfill that (Eph. 5:25). If she would have taken on the attitude *You haven't treated me the way the Bible says you should, so I'm justified in feeling this way!* do you see where this would go? Love, mercy, and grace make for much better relationships than just giving someone other what they deserve!

Chapter Two

Angry Brats

Angry people are self-centered! As a young man, my brother had a problem with losing his temper. After throwing a fit, he'd always say, "I'm sorry! If I had known what I was doing would hurt you, I wouldn't have done it." I heard that line hundreds of times growing up. What he meant was, "While angry, I didn't consider you or anyone else. I was all wrapped up in myself and how what had happened affected me." Talk about selfish!

Anger also manifests inwardly through self-pity, depression, and emotional wounds. Whenever hurt, your flesh wants to magnify the pain and focus on self. However, you can stop 90 percent of your depression, sorrow, and wounding by loving others. How does it work? Lack of concern for self helps immunize you against hurts!

As God's redeemed children, self provides an inviting beachhead for the devil's invasion plans. It's his preferred landing zone! Where the Enemy reigns, self is exalted as all-important. Self-preservation, even at the expense of anyone and everyone else, seems to our flesh like a virtue worthy of respect. But it's not so in God's kingdom! If we defend that beachhead by dealing with self-centeredness, we'll defeat many of the satanic problems in our lives!

Perspective Is Powerful

God spoke to me recently in a powerful way while watching an anti-capital-punishment television program. But before I share with you what I learned, I want to give you a little perspective on what I believe. Personally, I believe the death penalty is both scriptural and beneficial if properly administered. Just as the threat of war serves as a deterrent to rogue international powers, the threat of capital punishment deters rogue individuals within society. As a veteran who has actively served in the warzone during a time of actual combat, I don't particularly like war. However, as a citizen, I appreciate living in the benefits gained and protected by our country's previous victories. If civil authorities didn't make use of the death penalty, many more innocent lives would be needlessly devastated through the unrestrained selfish actions of a few malicious people!

As I watched the program, the spotlight shined on a certain man imprisoned for rape and murder. The television cameras zoomed in on his sad, lonely face before panning out to reveal the tall cement walls caging him there on death row. Pity rose within my heart as I saw images of the actual execution room and sensed the imminence of his death. Surely, this was a tragic situation!

Baby pictures and a cute little boy riding a stick horse paraded across the screen. I wondered, *How could such innocence grow up to commit these terrible crimes?* Sexual abuse and molestation entered the picture. At a very young age, he was already making the rounds at correctional institutions. It became increasingly clear just how many strikes this kid had lined up against him early in life. Everything had gone wrong—horribly wrong!

Like everyone else watching, I was tempted to feel sorry for this guy. Parts of the narration echoed in my head—"He never really had a chance!" My emotions had been skillfully manipulated through the presentation. The desire to see this man suffer for what he had done had diminished.

Then the Lord asked me, "What would happen if they also showed the baby pictures of the girl he had raped and murdered? What if they told the story of how she grew up, and then discussed her future plans?"

I thought to myself, *Perhaps this girl was a Christian who had wonderful dreams for a godly future. Maybe she even planned to marry a wholesome guy. Then some pervert forced himself upon her for self-gratification. After the rape, he murdered her trying to cover things up!* My feelings immediately swung from pity to righteous anger! The television program's sympathetic audience would have easily turned into an outraged vigilante posse if they had seen the girl's side of the story too. Why? Response is dependent upon perspective!

Your point of view dictates your emotions! It's dangerous to look at everything from a selfish standpoint: "Look what they are doing to me! Everybody has done me wrong!" Guess what? Every day of your life, self has ample opportunity to get rubbed the wrong way. If you are more concerned about others, then anger can't control you. Quit being self-centered and you won't get mad when unpleasant things happen. Why? You'll be thinking of the other person. Perspective is powerful!

You Were Born Selfish!

Human beings are selfish creatures by nature. As a newborn baby, you came into this world self-centered. Mom labored several hours for you to safely arrive. She was very tired and had been living in a degree of discomfort for quite some time. Perhaps even a couple of nights had passed since she had gotten some good rest…but hey, you didn't care! Immediately upon arrival, you announced your demands through that powerful cry—waaaah!

This continued as your parents took you home and got used to you. Anytime you felt you had a need, Mommy had better be there, or you'd start letting her know: "Feed me now! I need a new diaper. Hold me! I don't want to take a bath. I'm tired!" You were the very center of the universe! Nobody else existed unless they somehow met your needs. That's expected and acceptable behavior for a baby, but not for a twenty-, forty-, or sixty-year-old believer. You ought to know by now that there are other people in your world!

Aisle Nine

Biblical parenting involves dealing with your children's self-centeredness. Life's not about being served all the time! Children need to learn that it's in giving that they actually receive. They must be trained to serve others well. Did your parents impart this into your life? Are you building it into your children?

Most parents have a tough time addressing their children's self-centeredness because they have never really dealt with their own. In the heat of the moment, not correcting Junior often seems easier on Mom or Dad's flesh.

A woman is busy grocery shopping with her toddler. Right in the middle of aisle nine, the child boldly declares, "I want that!"

Calmly but firmly, Mom replies, "No, son. You can't have it."

Back and forth they go. His voice rises higher and higher until he screams, "I WANT THAT!" Seeing the need to add more pressure, the toddler throws himself on the floor and continues his temper tantrum.

Do you know what most self-centered parents do? They give in to the child because of their own selfishness. To get unwanted attention off of self ("Everybody's looking at me!"), the parent satisfies the child instead of bringing godly correction. When this happens, Junior's self has just been reinforced. He learns that self can get anything if self is willing to throw a fit!

Are You an Adult Brat?

Are you a thirty-, fifty-, or even seventy-year-old brat—still throwing temper tantrums to get your own way? Think about it! Do you pout and withdraw from relationships in an attempt to "punish" others? Do you persecute people until they come crawling back to you in repentance? Are you a "blaster"—soundly giving everyone within earshot a piece of your mind? Or do slyness, patience, and subtlety better suit your retaliatory taste, since "revenge is best served cold!" No matter how you slice it up, it's still self-centeredness!

You need to recognize your anger for what it really is—self-centeredness in action. From the Father's perspective, all these adult methods amount to nothing more than your kicking and screaming on the floor of aisle nine. Friend, it's time to grow up!

Chapter Three

Sober Heroes

Nobody has fully conquered self. In fact, most people haven't even dealt with it on a conscious level! God doesn't just kill you and remove self out of His way. He expects you to exercise self-control. Learning to deny self and exalt Him on a daily basis is foundational for your spiritual growth.

Have you ever consciously dealt with your own selfishness? What do you do when someone comes against you? Who do you think of first? Do you consider the other person, or are you consumed with defending yourself?

Who's the Meekest of Them All?

Moses dealt with self. When people blasted him with accusations, he immediately fell to his face and prayed for them. Why? He knew they were in big trouble with God! Instead of defending himself, Moses called on the Lord to show his offenders mercy.

"Miriam and Aaron spake against Moses because of the Ethiopian woman whom he had married: for he had married an Ethiopian woman" (Num. 12:1).

Moses was Middle Eastern, and his wife was Black. His brother and sister spoke out against him because of this interracial marriage.

"And they said, Hath the LORD indeed spoken only by Moses? hath he not spoken also by us? And the LORD heard it" (Num. 12:2). In other words, Aaron and Miriam quit esteeming Moses and began criticizing him because he'd done something wrong in their opinion. They openly challenged his leadership, declaring, "You aren't the only one God speaks through. We are His vessels too!"

The next statement is awesome! "(Now the man Moses was very meek, above all the men which were upon the face of the earth.)" (Num. 12:3). The Holy Spirit directed Moses himself to record in the Word for all time this evaluation of his own humility: "I am the meekest man on the face of the earth!" Isn't that amazing? Only the Lord knows how many millions of people were alive back then, and Moses was the meekest of them all!

Moses cried out for mercy on behalf of his two offending siblings (Num 12:13), and the Lord granted his request. What an example! Moses lived life more conscious of God and others than of himself.

The Lord's been building this same attitude in me. I haven't arrived yet, but I left years ago! On several occasions, I've been so consciously overwhelmed by His presence that I became almost oblivious to the world around me. I felt like Moses coming down the mountain with God's glory on his face. Wherever I looked, all I could see was Him whom I loved! This focus enabled me to be supernaturally protected in the midst of some very dangerous situations.

Overrun!

Two decades passed before I realized the miracle God had performed for me in Vietnam. I never could relate to the trauma that other American soldiers experienced because of their involvement in the war. I was fired on and could have been killed in action on many occasions, but I came home a hundred times stronger inside and a thousand times more in love with Jesus. Serving my country as a soldier in Vietnam was one of the best experiences of my life! Therefore, I didn't bother reading anything about it until twenty years later.

I was given a book containing the combat testimonies of twelve former servicemen. Three of the guys were in my division, two were in Vietnam the same time I was, and one wrote his account of a fire support base that was overrun by the Vietcong.

Our LZ (landing zone) was a fire support station on the border of Laos. Located in what seemed like the middle of nowhere, I could see the Ho Chi Minh Trail from our position. The station only occupied about as much real estate as an old-fashioned camp meeting tent.

We took an average of twenty mortar rounds per hour in this small area. Every few minutes, the scream of an incoming projectile sent us scurrying for cover. I arrived just two days before the hill was overrun.

As I read this man's account, the Lord opened my eyes to see my LZ overrun from an unbeliever's perspective. Even though I didn't know him, the author and I had been there at exactly the same time. The stark terror he experienced in that moment had caused nightmares to plague him on and off ever since.

I just remember being head over heels in love with Jesus! Even though fear, death, and danger pressed in on every side, God's presence enveloped me in a supernatural bubble. I was and wasn't there—both at the same time!

As the 5,000 North Vietnamese soldiers surrounding us charged, all I could do was pray, "Father, those guys don't know You! I hope I don't have to kill any of them!" My thoughts weren't, *What's going to happen to me?* I was too busy interceding for those advancing enemy troops! I was close enough to see the muzzle fire from their weapons, but fear couldn't touch me. I was out of myself, praying for someone else. "God, please touch them—somehow!" Fear can only affect you when you're thinking about yourself.

Heroes

Heroes put others first. An airplane crashed into a river several winters ago near Washington, D.C. Different individuals jumped into the freezing cold water and rescued passengers who had survived the impact. Reporters later interviewed these heroes, asking, "Didn't you think of yourself? What would have happened to your spouse and children if you had lost your life?" Each one answered, "I didn't think about that. All I could focus on was saving those people!"

When thrust into an emergency situation, heroes willingly risks their own lives to save others'. None of these hesitated on the bank of that freezing-cold river, thinking, *These people need me, but so does my family!* Concern for the passengers in distress outweighed self. If they had been more focused on themselves than on those who needed their help, they wouldn't have done it!

Spirit-Filled and Selfish

This message opposes much of today's "popular Christianity." My heart breaks to see so many Spirit-filled believers acting just as selfishly as the world! Drawn into the full Gospel message for what they thought they could get out of it, their real "god" is self. It's time to confront wrong motives!

God is no vending machine—He's Lord and King! You can't just insert a coin, push His button, and take out whatever you want, whenever you want it. Prosperity wasn't provided for you to consume it upon your own lusts. Don't trample the healing blood of Jesus by running right back to the same old vice that destroyed you before. That's just ignorant, immature, and self-centered! Of course, the Father has provided for His children's every need—but child, it's time to grow up and stop treating Him so selfishly!

"Seek ye first the kingdom of God, and his righteousness; and all these things shall be added unto you" (Matt. 6:33). Your necessities are added to you as byproducts of seeking first the King and His kingdom. Faith is to believe for other people's needs to be met through you. It was never intended to be used primarily for self! If you concentrate on blessing others, you'll be blessed in the process. The question is, where is your focus?

Void of Speculative Imaginations?

Sobriety is one of God's qualifications for ministers. "This is a true saying, If a man desire the office of a bishop, he desireth a good work. A bishop then must be...sober" (1 Tim. 3:1-2). When I became an elder, I sought the Lord for what this looked like in everyday life. Since "not given to wine" is specifically mentioned in the next verse, I saw that sobriety had more to do with my attitude. When I looked in the dictionary, "being void of speculative imaginations" stood out to me the most. So, I asked Him, "Father, what does 'being void of speculative imaginations' mean?" His answer came one day quite unexpectedly!

By that time in my ministry, I already traveled regularly to preach in various cities. The Lord has always blessed me with special friends and Gospel partners wherever I go. If I'm scheduled to minister anywhere near them, their attendance can be counted on. I praise God for such committed partners and friends!

Pondering sobriety, I began a series of meetings near where one of these "old faithful" couples lived. I watched for them the whole first evening, but they didn't show. Since their absence was out of character, my mind raced back to the last time I'd seen them. I remembered calling them out of the crowd with a very specific prophecy. It wasn't just a regular, general kind of word. I either nailed it or blew it! In ministering that prophetic word, I'd made myself really vulnerable.

While reflecting on this, the thought came, *I must have missed it with that prophecy. Those people probably think I'm a false prophet now. I bet they've disregarded all of the good they ever received from me!* By the time self was done, I had visualized this couple out campaigning against me, proclaiming, "Andrew Wommack is of the devil!" I came close to the point of wanting to punch them in the nose!

The very next evening, this couple came to the meeting and explained, "We are so sorry we couldn't make it last night. A death in our family kept us out of town all week long. We never would have missed your meeting!"

At that very moment, the Lord revealed to me what "speculative imaginations" are. I had stirred myself up over something completely imagined in my head. Unfounded in either reality or truth, this pure speculation had begun with my wondering why they hadn't come and spiraled downward due to selfishness. Praise God I didn't punch them in the nose!

Brothers and sisters, lay down your speculative imaginations and take up a sober mind. Humble yourselve and believe the best of others. Pray for those who offend you. Love God—don't just try to use Him! You are more blessed in giving than in receiving, so if you use your faith to meet the needs of others, yours will be abundantly met too! Let's continue maturing in Him!

Chapter Four

My Religious Humility

I am amazed at how easily some people take offense! I'm usually polite and friendly to the hundreds of people I see each week, but once in a while, my mind may be somewhere else when someone says "hello." Annoyed, they'll persist in asking me questions like, "What's the matter. Is something wrong?" The truth is, they were offended because I didn't respond the way they thought I should. I've seen people offended because their pastor didn't call last week, or he greeted the person next to them and forgot to shake their hand. This sort of immaturity happens more frequently than you might think, and it's rooted in self-centeredness.

People who love God more than themselves don't just fall apart when situations turn out differently than they expected. That's why Jesus asked the disciples, "Why are you so upset?" (John 14:28, paraphrase mine). They were focused on His leaving more than rejoicing in His going to the Father. The disciples embraced their "crisis" over His joy, because of self-centeredness.

Does your marriage feel like a crisis to you? Your spouse isn't your problem—you are! Divorcing that mate and getting a new one won't solve anything. You'll face the same problem, no matter who your mate is, because you can't divorce yourself! Wherever you go, whomever you're with, self will be there too. The devil may even use your spouse to give you a hard time, but it really doesn't matter what they do. Until you deal with your own selfish state of mind, nobody can please you.

A Separated but Selfish Life

I failed miserably dealing with my own self-centeredness. The religion I was brought up in taught against self, constantly reinforcing dying to self and crucifying self. Although there's some truth to what they said, the recommended "cure" only made the "sickness" worse.

I remember being given pen and paper and told to list every sin I'd ever committed. Even though I've never spoken a cuss word, smoked a cigarette, tasted liquor or drunk coffee in all my life (not that drinking coffee is sin—you can stand on Mark 16:18 for that: "If they drink any deadly thing, it shall not hurt them"), it wasn't long before I'd filled up both sides of the paper and asked for another sheet!

Seeing all those sins listed crushed me but did nothing to cure my selfishness. I'd mope around all day long, head hung low, confessing "Woe is me, I'm undone" and singing "Such a worm as I" with conviction. I felt completely worthless and considered myself the very scum of the earth!

By the time I finished high school, I'd marinated in religion for sixteen years. My feelings of inferiority made me feel so bad that I couldn't even look a person in the face and talk to them! I had the lowest self-esteem of anyone I knew, yet I was operating in just as much pride as everyone else. Since I didn't exalt myself, I thought I was safe. I didn't realize that self-debasement was pride too! Either way, it's just self-centeredness.

Truly Humble

Most people who call themselves "timid" or "shy" are really just being prideful. Low self-esteem causes self to dominate their thoughts. Even the prospect of testifying in front of others about what God has done in their lives causes fear to race through their minds: *What will people think of me? Will I make a fool of myself?*

I remember a man who spoke with me after a service in Pueblo, Colorado. He said, "I don't have any pride. I have just the opposite—low self-esteem." I responded by telling him that his low self-esteem was really just another form of pride. It's the result of focusing on yourself as compared to others and then coming to the conclusion that you just don't measure up, and everyone around you knows it. It's still just all about you.

I had to work through this same thing when I first started ministering. God used a wise man to set me free. He said, "Andy, if you ever get more concerned about the people you are ministering to than you are about yourself and what they think of yourself, God will use you!" Today I don't really care what anyone thinks of me, as long as I can get God's point across clearly.

Self, compared to Jesus, is a non-issue to the truly humble. They don't consider self any higher or lower than what His Word says. God-centered people will do something to their own detriment at the Lord's direction. They'll also bless themselves whenever He leads. Either way, self doesn't hinder them from obeying the Father they love!

Gone Fishin'

Many people still believe that to debase self is humility and to exalt self is pride. James 4:10 contradicts this religious notion by revealing who God wants to exalt: "Humble yourselves in the sight of the Lord, and he shall lift you up." What happens when people humble themselves, and God starts to exalt them? The truly humble will let Him do it, but the proud won't. They're too concerned about what others think.

Self-centered people can't handle positive feedback either. After giving an anointed word or singing an inspired song, they respond, "It was all Jesus. Don't give me any praise, because I'm nothin'!" Without realizing it, they drew all the attention back to self! A humble person would answer encouraging words, saying, "Thanks. Praise God for Jesus!"

False humility also fishes for compliments: "I really don't have a very good voice, but the Lord says, 'Make a joyful noise.' Please pray for me while I try to sing!" They knock themselves down hoping to hook someone into lifting them up. That's just pride in action!

Stinkin' Thinkin'

I resurrected self every morning while trying my best to kill it. Strapping myself into an imaginary electric chair, I confessed all of the sins I thought I'd recently committed—"Pride!" "Arrogance!" "Not studying the Word!"—on and on it went. After an hour of "executing" everything I could think of, I'd spent my entire devotional time focused on myself.

Religious ways of dealing with selfishness only make you religiously humble. Afterward, you're still so full of self that when the Lord says "Go lay your hands on the sick and they'll recover," you immediately focus on your limitations and respond, "Who, me?" God's not able to use you in His power, because of your own stinkin' thinkin'!

"I Love You, Jamie!"

Love for another overcomes self. When God supernaturally put Jamie and I together, five years had passed since I stopped dating. The Lord had told me that His way of finding my mate would be much better than the world's. Out of love for Jesus and my future bride, I believed Him.

When I announced my engagement to the crew at work, they couldn't believe I'd remain honest, upright, and moral while preparing to marry such a beautiful young lady. It was hard enough on their heads that Jamie and I were engaged before holding hands or going on a date, but these heathen fellows didn't think I'd stay the course. They judged me according to their party lifestyle (sleeping with different women each night, getting drunk, etc.), knowing full well I had never done anything immoral like that. Constantly, they provoked me in attempt after attempt to "prove" that their distorted perceptions of me were true. The boss, my best friend, and I just kept witnessing to them whenever we could. However, all this harassment made working as a cement finisher downright miserable at times!

Every morning upon arrival, the crew sang the same old chorus: "Mr. Goody-Goody, what did you do last night? Were you out playing licky-face? What time did you come in?" Therefore, I decided never again to bring up the topic of Jamie at work. It just gave them too much ammunition!

Then one day, I stood beside a bay window watching the reflection from the sun on the freshly poured cement. The beauty of the sunlight hitting the water in just the right way caused my thoughts to center on my wife-to-be. Temporarily oblivious to my surroundings, I started crooning, "I love you, Jamie! I love you, Jamie!" I was wonderfully lost in the sweetness of my bride-to-be. However, my short-lived bliss came to a screeching halt as I noticed all these other smiling faces materializing beside mine in the reflection. The entire crew stood there listening as I crooned one last time, "I love you, Jamie!" Immediately, they unleashed on me with a fury!

I would never have said that in front of all those guys if I'd been in control! But I was smitten, and my loving awareness of Jamie superseded my awareness of me. Because of that, I actually did something that was not in the best interest of self. Love had truly overcome! Self-awareness was gone when I fell more in love with someone else than myself. And that is truly the only way to overcome self-awareness.

Chapter Five

Selfish Soul-Winner

I was afraid to witness before I truly fell in love with Jesus. I forced myself to share my faith out of religious duty. I even pushed myself to make ten extra visits above the weekly visitation quota. Impressed, the church asked me to take others on my rounds and disciple them in "soul winning." Even though I did this with some degree of success, fear overwhelmed me inside because I was an introvert. Basically, I was self-centered and scared to talk with people. On the way up to the door, my silent prayer consisted of, "O God, please let there be no one home!"

How did I do it? I reminded myself what it felt like to receive recognition, honor, and awards for leading people to the Lord. At seventeen years old, I regularly saw more "decisions for Christ" than my pastor! Every Sunday, the church leaders reported my weekly "head count" and congratulated me in front of the whole congregation. I used this as motivation during the hours I spent praying and psyching myself up before witnessing. Selfishness enabled me to overcome my fear.

Manipulated!

Most churches manipulate you to witness by appealing to self. They sing these old hymns about standing before God with bloodstained hands and no souls to present Him. Preachers warn of a "Judgment Seat" where your unsaved neighbor will stand beside you sticking his brimstone-scorched, still smoking finger in your face and demanding, "Why didn't you tell me about the Lord?" When these songs and stories are used, altars overflow with people desiring to "witness." Why does this work? Self doesn't want to suffer embarrassment: "I'm not going to stand before Almighty God empty handed on that day!" So, what do you do? You witness to people not because you love them but because you love yourself.

Religion promotes self. How often have you heard, "Give so self can receive! Do you want to prosper? Give generously into my offering and the Lord will bless it back to you a hundredfold"? Some of you have plunked down hundreds, even thousands, of dollars into offerings and have yet to see the return. Do you know why? You gave apart from God's selfless, unconditional love. Your true motivation was self-centered because your heart attitude depended solely on whether or not you saw the return. The Word says that even if you give all your goods to feed the poor, without love, it profits you nothing (1 Cor. 13:3). The motive behind your gift is more important than your gift. God's kind of love is not self-centered!

Overwhelmed by His Love

On March 23, 1968, I had an encounter with God that changed my life forever—I found out how much Jesus loved me! Immediately, my world turned upside down for four-and-a-half beautiful months as the Lord completely occupied my thoughts. I forgot all about the horse that I rode every day. Whether it had been fed or was still alive, I didn't know. I also forgot about the television programs that I watched four to five hours a day. They never even crossed my mind! Except for an hour or two each night, my excitement also kept me from sleeping. I'd stand and read until I passed out and hit the floor. Then I'd wake up and do it again. I fell so in love with God that He revolutionized my entire life!

I started witnessing to everything that moved! Gone were the prayers of "O God, let there be nobody home!" I quit those visitations on Thursday nights and started talking to people wherever and whenever. Knocking on over one hundred doors a day, I shared Christ in homes, stores, gas stations, and restaurants. Not once did I fear what they might say about me, because now I genuinely cared about lost people. I wanted everyone to know and experience the Lord's awesome love!

Love Jesus more than yourself! Fall in love with Him, and you'll quit thinking about self. When you witness to people, you'll be bold and full of His love for them. Confidence will rise in your heart as you recognize what He's done in your life. God's love changes everything!

Beware of Dogs

Shortly after this, we divided our city into sections and began knocking on hundreds of doors. I started in the wealthiest part of town, which wasn't smart, but I didn't know any better. Doors slammed in our faces one after another. We started by asking the simple question "Are you a Christian?" but discovered very quickly that people didn't know what a Christian was. They answered, "Of course I'm a Christian! I'm not Buddhist or Hindu, so I must be a Christian." Some actually pulled coins out of their pockets and explained, "See right there? It says, 'In God We Trust.' I've got to be a Christian!" They didn't understand about a born-again experience.

One day I determined in my heart to talk to the lady in a particular house. Since I was tired of doors slamming in my face, I decided to change my approach. When she answered the door, I loudly declared, "Praise God, I've found a Christian!"

She looked straight at me and asked, "What makes you think I'm a Christian?"

Seizing my opportunity, I continued, "Well, you have a scripture out here hanging on your fence."

She opened the door, stepped out onto the porch, and inquired, "What do you mean?"

Immediately turning to Philippians 3:2, I read, "Beware of dogs…" and just kept right on going! I finished the rest of that chapter before she shut the door in my face.

What a difference in me! I was using gimmicks and doing anything I could just to talk to people about the Lord. Why? I was more concerned about them than me.

The best things that have ever happened to me occurred when I laid self aside and just gave my life for somebody else. So what if they hate you. So what if your spouse is upset. Sacrifice yourself! It's more blessed to give than to receive. Finding out that you aren't the center of the universe is fun!

You're Better Off than You Think!

Living in the U.S.A., you are better off than you think. I visited a millionaire's home in India and was surprised to find that almost every American house I'd seen was cleaner and nicer. How much more do you need? Is God really the one leading you to buy that bigger, newer, more expensive house? Just checking!

Some Americans have developed a welfare mentality, saying "This government owes me a living!" Wrong! People don't owe you anything. Pardon me if that ruffles your feathers, but you're alive to be productive and to give. You aren't here just to live off society. Change your mindset! Quit being so self-centered. Stop sitting there soaking up other people's resources and start being productive!

Some people may need government assistance for a short period of time, until they can get back on their feet, but not generation after generation. If you are capable of working, you should! I remember making over $500 a month in the late 1960s as a high school kid delivering newspapers. If you can't provide for yourself better than welfare, you've already got one foot in the grave. Anybody can beat welfare when God is your source.He'll lead you step by step into a more prosperous life!

Gimme, Gimme!

Self-centered people constantly think, *What can I get? What can I receive from this relationship? What can this church do for me? Why haven't they done this? Why haven't they done that?* Instead, people should be thinking, *How can I be a blessing? How can God meet their need through me? How can I help make this church what God wants it to be? What do I have to contribute?*

Stop pointing the finger at your family and start asking, "What can I do for my spouse? How can I be a blessing to each member of my household?" Quit thinking, *They don't deserve it*, because you don't either! Settle the score, call it even, and start over. Try to out-give each other!

Serve your church and bless your family, but don't do it with selfish motives. Treating your spouse like royalty in order to be treated like royalty is self-centeredness all over again! Wherever you are, whomever you're with, ask yourself, "How can I be a blessing?"

Chapter Six

God's Unselfish Love

God is love! Jesus Christ gave His life as much for Adolf Hitler as He did for you. Adolf may not have accepted the Lord, but Jesus loved him. In fact, Jesus doesn't love Spirit-filled believers any more than those who aren't. Spirit-filled believers might experience Him in greater ways, but He wants to baptize all those other Christians in the Holy Spirit too! The same love is available to all because love is His very nature.

God is an extravagant giver! He didn't have to lay down His life for us. The Father, Son, and Holy Spirit weren't going to fall apart if mankind wasn't redeemed. He could have chosen to wipe us all out and create a brand-new race, but He didn't. Christ generously sacrificed Himself for us—the helpless, pathetic sinners that we were. What an awesome display of unconditional love!

Carnal love pales in comparison. When we "love" others based on their performance, we betray our shallow understanding and experience of God's kind of love. His attitude says, "I choose to love you. I don't care if you hate Me, spit on Me, or despitefully use Me. My mind's made up. I love you!" As the light of this relentless love first dawned on my soul, I prayed, "Lord, let Your unconditional love flow through me!" I had no idea how liberating the answers to this prayer would be!

Forgiveness in Pritchett

I used to pastor a small church in Pritchett, Colorado. At that church, the congregation and I grated on each other's nerves. Back in those days, I'd fight at the drop of a hat and drop my hat to get to fight. My pastoral motto was simply "This is the way it is, and if you don't like it—there's the door!" I realize now that we should have used more wisdom in dealing with each other, but we didn't. Even though we had our problems, God still confirmed His Word through many notable miracles, including a man being raised from the dead.

Less than a year after I arrived, several people in the church tried to run me off. Different individuals lied and publicly opposed me in various ways. They accused me of stealing money from the church, when I wasn't even receiving a salary! To this day, a certain person has threatened to kill me if I ever set foot on their property. Without discussing the details of all the other matters, these people basically chose to turn around and stab me in the back after all I tried to do for them. I forgave and decided to walk in love anyway.

The fellow who had become one of my best friends ended up doing everything he could to hurt me. I caught him on the telephone once telling someone that I was of the devil and other terrible things. When confronted, he accused me of being a crook and wouldn't agree with anything. As an elder, he stirred things up and led the group who tried to run me out of the church. I just gave all this to the Lord and forgave him from the bottom of my heart!

Barely a week had passed when Jamie and I went for a drive. I was in the habit of stopping in and chatting with this brother at his service station. It was something I enjoyed, so I parked, went inside, and tried talking with him for a while. Getting back into the car, I told Jamie, "Something's wrong! I don't know what it is, but he's just not the same!"

Jamie looked at me and exclaimed, "What are you talking about?"

"Well, something's wrong with him," I answered. "He didn't treat me normal."

Incredulously, she looked at me and asked, "Don't you remember?" Jamie had to rehash the entire situation from the week before!

I had forgiven him to such a degree that after spending fifteen minutes with this guy, I was still totally perplexed over his lack of friendliness! Literally, I had let the issue go and had forgotten all about it, choosing instead to love him with God's unconditional love. Now, that's freedom!

You're Only Hurting Yourself

You're only hurting yourself by staying mad, holding grudges, and harboring bitterness. It's not harming the other person or improving your situation. God didn't create you with a capacity to carry such things. Nursing wounds and using your imagination to "punish" others only wrecks your relationships and will eventually kill you. "To me belongeth vengeance," says the Lord (Deut. 32:35). Your heavenly defender has much better ways to take care of what concerns you. Don't try to avenge yourself—forgive!

I've had a nationally known minister accuse me of leading a cult. Throwing the full weight of their organization against me, they passionately declared that I was "slicker than Jim Jones!" Apparently, this cult leader was the best "faith"-type preacher they had ever heard of back then. Both the minister and their following used all of their power and influence in a concerted attempt to subvert my ministry.

I forgave and loved this person. Since then, we've ministered on the same radio station, held meetings together, and even hugged. More than once, I've sent people to their church and given money toward their projects. I can honestly tell you that I'm not holding anything against this person or their ministry. Instead of being bound by un-forgiveness, anger, and bitterness, my full attention remains unhindered and focused on the Lord!

God-Consciousness Restored

God created you to live life focused on Him. He purposed from the very beginning that your "God-consciousness" should always supercede your "self-consciousness." Adam and Eve enjoyed constant awareness of their Creator until they ate the forbidden fruit. That's when their attention fell from Him to themselves.

Through the Last Adam's sacrifice and the outpouring of the Holy Spirit, everything you need to live in continual God-consciousness has already been provided. You can choose to leave self-centeredness behind and return your focus to the one you were created for—Love Himself.

Who will you choose—God or self? Only you can decide!

Chapter Seven

A Living Sacrifice

"I beseech you therefore, brethren, by the mercies of God, that ye present your bodies a living sacrifice, holy, acceptable unto God, which is your reasonable service" (Rom. 12:1). Present yourself a living sacrifice today by humbling yourself, rejecting self as "lord," and laying on God's altar. Then, call for His heavenly fire to come and consume you! In light of all He's done for you, this is your reasonable service.

The only problem with living sacrifices is they tend to crawl off the altar. Even if you make this commitment in your heart right now, you'll have to renew it again tomorrow, next week, and next month. Choosing to love Jesus more than self is a continual, life decision. You can't pray once and deal with self forever. It just doesn't work that way. As long as you're here on earth, you must continually choose to "stay on the altar" by reckoning self as dead and submitting to the authority of the Holy Spirit. If you don't, self will find a way to rear its ugly head again real soon!

The Lord wants you void of self even more than you do. He's inviting you to consciously begin this life commitment today. Throw yourself wide open to God, and let the Holy Spirit minister this truth deep in your heart!

Matured by His Word

In His goodness, God sends His Word—not sickness, disease, or poverty—to correct and mature His beloved children. By His Word, you are thoroughly furnished unto all good works (2 Tim. 3:16-17). God's Word has come to you today! Will you humble yourself and act in faith on what He's spoken?

The very fact that you have read this far tells me something: You are probably someone whom other people call "good." Most of the time, you have good attitudes and good desires. You may even be active in your local church in many ways. However, be honest with yourself: Are you winning the day-to-day battle with self? I'm fully aware that you haven't "arrived" yet, but have you left?

Most people have never consciously dealt with self. Is that true of you? Perhaps this is the first time a message from God's Word on this topic has ever been presented to you. Maybe you have denied yourself a little in some areas, but overall, self has remained your true king. Deep down in your heart, are you still the center of the universe? Are you an adult brat who throws temper tantrums—sophisticated or not? Do you consume upon yourself every resource that comes your way? Has it really sunk into your heart that there's someone more important than you?

The Holy Spirit is leading you to make a particular response right now in light of what He's been revealing. Whether you have consciously done this before or not, God wants you to deal with self faithfully from now on. It's a process that will continue for the rest of your life!

I used to think that the Apollo spacecraft traveled directly to the moon in a straight line. Then I met Jim Irwin, one of the astronauts who walked on the moon. He said, "We made course corrections every ten minutes for the entire flight. We just kept checking where we were against where we were going and adjusted accordingly until we arrived."

Conditions and circumstances are always changing, giving opportunity for self to rise up and gain control again in your life. When you begin to deal with self-centeredness honestly, you've left the launch pad. However, as conditions .change, there will be many course corrections you must make to keep self in submission. Have you left yet? Are you making regular course adjustments?

A Hypocrite Humbled

On Saturday night, March 23, 1968, I had an encounter with God that changed my life forever. You may have heard me tell this before, but I believe it will help you overcome self-centeredness in your life. I was raised in a Christian home and born again at the tender age of eight. I avoided going through the rebellious phase associated with adolescence but went the opposite direction and became a modern-day "Pharisee" instead. I actually believed that through my own righteousness and good works, I could develop a closer relationship with the Lord.

As usual, I met with my friends for intercessory prayer on what I thought would be just another Saturday night. However, as I listened to my friend pray, bitterness rose up strong in my heart: *He's talking to God as if He were his friend! Why can't I do that?* Right then, the Lord held a mirror before me, and I saw my reflection clearly for the first time. I didn't like what I saw. The person in the mirror was a hypocrite—much like the religious leaders Jesus rebuked. I was doing good things for man's approval and to earn God's love.

Immediately, I began to confess my self-centeredness along with any other sin I could think of. I fully expected the wrath of God to fall. Instead, His presence flooded me with unconditional love! When I was at my absolute worst, God's love consumed me! Instantly, I fell deeply in love with the Lord and forgot all about myself for the next four months. During that time, I wasn't even aware of my eating or sleeping because I was so completely taken up with Him!

When you become more conscious of God than yourself, self-centeredness disappears. Humble yourself, become a living sacrifice, and much of your grief will come to an end!

Present Yourself!

Pray this out loud in front of God, yourself, and the devil. For maximum effect, ask your spouse or someone close to listen and agree as you pray (self won't like that, but it's good for you). Humble yourself, reject self as "lord," and lay upon God's altar. Then call on the Lord's fire from heaven to consume you—a living sacrifice!

Father, I choose to humble myself today. I want to be more conscious of You than I am of me. I see now how selfish I've been. Therefore, I wholeheartedly renounce self-centeredness and choose to turn from it now!

Forgive me for blaming circumstances and other people, for being depressed because I didn't get something, and for being so consumed with myself. Father, I've allowed "self" to be "god" in my life—please forgive me!

Change me from within so only You are God! I'm not sure how, but I'm willing! I want You to be Lord over every part of my life.

Father, I place myself upon Your altar as a living sacrifice. I'll obey anything You ask me to do. Please help me love You more than I love myself. Consume me in the fire of Your heavenly love from this day forward, in the name of Jesus Christ, my King! Amen.

If you prayed this from your heart, God has faithfully begun His work. Go ahead and express your love to Jesus. Use your own words to praise and exalt Him. Consider His goodness in your life, and thank Him for changing you from the inside out.

Begin practicing His presence wherever you are and acknowledging Him throughout the day. Your love for and awareness of the Lord will increase. Then what used to be a "crisis" won't even faze you as you pass through life's adversities alive and prospering in Him! Glory to Jesus!

How to Receive Jesus

Choosing to receive Jesus Christ as your Lord and Savior is the most important decision you'll ever make!

God's Word promises, "That if thou shalt confess with thy mouth the Lord Jesus, and shalt believe in thine heart that God hath raised him from the dead, thou shalt be saved. For with the heart man believeth unto righteousness; and with the mouth confession is made unto salvation" (Rom. 10:9-10). "For whosoever shall call upon the name of the Lord shall be saved" (Rom. 10:13).

By His grace, God has already done everything to provide salvation. Your part is simply to believe and receive.

Pray out loud, *"Jesus, I confess that You are my Lord and Savior. I believe in my heart that God raised You from the dead. By faith in Your Word, I receive salvation now. Thank You for saving me!"*

The very moment you commit your life to Jesus Christ, the truth of His Word instantly comes to pass in your spirit. Now that you're born again, there's a brand-new you!

Please contact me and let me know that you've prayed to receive Jesus as your Savior or to be filled with the Holy Spirit. I would like to rejoice with you and help you understand more fully what has taken place in your life. I'll send you a free gift that will help you understand and grow in your new relationship with the Lord. *Welcome to your new life!*

How to Receive
the Holy Spirit

As His child, your loving heavenly Father wants to give you the supernatural power you need to live this new life.

"For every one that asketh receiveth; and he that seeketh findeth; and to him that knocketh it shall be opened...how much more shall your heavenly Father give the Holy Spirit to them that ask him?" (Luke 11:10-13).

All you have to do is ask, believe, and receive!

Pray, *"Father, I recognize my need for Your power to live this new life. Please fill me with Your Holy Spirit. By faith, I receive it right now! Thank You for baptizing me. Holy Spirit, You are welcome in my life!"*

Congratulations! Now you're filled with God's supernatural power.

Some syllables from a language you don't recognize will rise up from your heart to your mouth (1 Cor. 14:14). As you speak them out loud by faith, you're releasing God's power from within and building yourself up in your spirit (1 Cor. 14:4). You can do this whenever and wherever you like.

It doesn't really matter whether you felt anything or not when you prayed to receive the Lord and His Spirit. If you believed in your heart that you received, then God's Word promises that you did. **"Therefore I say unto you, What things soever ye desire, when ye pray, believe that ye receive them, and ye shall have them"** (Mark 11:24). God always honors His Word—believe it!

Please contact me and let me know that you've prayed to receive Jesus as your Savior or to be filled with the Holy Spirit. I would like to rejoice with you and help you understand more fully what has taken place in your life. I'll send you a free gift that will help you understand and grow in your new relationship with the Lord. *Welcome to your new life!*